Common Core Lessons & Activities: Westward Expansion

By Carole Marsh
Published by Gallopade International, Inc.

Printed in the U.S.A. (Peachtree City, Georgia)

TABLE OF CONTENTS

G: Includes Graphic Organizer
GO: Graphic Organizer is also available 8½" x 11" online download at www.gallopade.com/client/go
(numbers above correspond to the graphic organizer numbers online)

The Louisiana Purchase: Expansion and Exploration

Read the texts and answer the questions.

The Louisiana Purchase

After the Treaty of Paris of 1783, the United States controlled most of the land east of the Mississippi River. However, other countries occupied areas in North America as well. Great Britain occupied Canada, the Pacific Northwest, and land near the Great Lakes. Spain occupied Florida, what is now Mexico, and the southwestern U.S. France occupied the Louisiana Territory, which spread west from the Mississippi River to the Rocky Mountains.

In the early 1800s, the Mississippi River was a center of trade for British, French, and American frontiersmen. U.S. President Thomas Jefferson believed it was important for the U.S. to control the Mississippi River and the French port city of New Orleans. In 1801, Jefferson sent James Madison to France to negotiate buying New Orleans from the French emperor Napoleon Bonaparte.

Napoleon needed money for a war against Great Britain. As a result, Napoleon offered to sell the entire Louisiana Territory, giving up all French claims to land in North America. Thomas Jefferson believed expanding the nation's land westward would make the United States' economy stronger, so he accepted Napoleon's offer. In 1803, Congress purchased the Louisiana Territory for $15 million, doubling the land area of the United States. This land purchase opened the door to westward expansion, a defining theme of the 1800s in which the U.S. gained and settled land across the American West.

1. Which countries occupied North America in 1783?
2. Why was Thomas Jefferson interested in expanding the boundaries of the United States beyond the Mississippi River?
3. A. How did the Louisiana Purchase affect the United States?
   B. How did the Louisiana Purchase affect France?
4. A. Define westward expansion, as it is used in the text.
   B. What is the relationship between the Louisiana Purchase and westward expansion?

The Lewis and Clark Expedition

In 1804, Thomas Jefferson appointed Meriwether Lewis and William Clark to lead an expedition of nine men into the Louisiana Territory. Jefferson instructed Lewis and Clark to explore the Columbia River, which he thought might be a good trade route from the Missouri River to the Pacific Ocean.

During their journey, Lewis and Clark kept detailed journals describing the geography of the American West. They described plant and animal life people in the eastern U.S. had never seen before. They also wrote about their experiences with Native Americans they met on their journey.

Lewis and Clark's descriptions of abundant land, trees, and natural resources in the Oregon Territory (Oregon, Nevada, and Washington State) caused excitement in the East about the prospect of moving westward. Settlers desiring to move west saw the Louisiana and Oregon territories as a new frontier, a place to begin a new life and make a living off the land's many natural resources.

5. A. What is a synonym for expedition, as it is used in the text?
   B. Why did Thomas Jefferson order the Lewis and Clark expedition?
   C. List at least three effects of Lewis and Clark's expedition.

6. Use descriptions from the first text to identify each of the following sections on the map:

   _________ Louisiana Purchase ________The United States
   _________ Spanish Territory ________British Territory

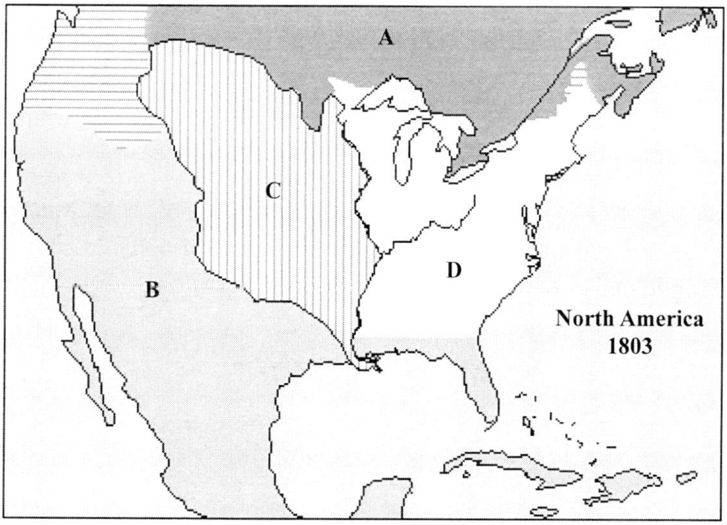

The Corps of Discovery

The Lewis and Clark expedition was formally called the "Corps of Discovery" and included 9 other recruits from the United States Army.

Read the texts and answer the questions.

"This forenoon we passed a large creek on the North side and a small river on the South. About 4 in the afternoon we passed another small river on the South side near the mouth of which some of the men discovered a large brown bear, and six of them went out to kill it. They fired at it; but having only wounded it, it made battle and was near seizing some of them, but they all fortunately escaped, and at length succeeded in dispatching it. These bears are very bold and ferocious; and very large and powerful. The natives say they have killed a number of their brave men."

—Excerpt from Patrick Gass' Journal on the Corps of Discovery

"Whilst I viewed those [Rocky] mountains, I felt a secret pleasure in finding myself so near the head of the... boundless Missouri [River]. But when I reflected on the difficulties which this snowy barrier would most probably throw in my way to the Pacific Ocean, and the sufferings and hardships of myself and the party in them, it in some measure counterbalanced the joy I had felt in the first moments in which I gazed on them. But, as I have always held it little short of criminality to anticipate evils, I will allow it to be a good, comfortable road until I am compelled to believe otherwise."

— Excerpt from William Clark's Journal on the Corps of Discovery

1. What types of information does the first text provide? Why?
2. In your opinion, is hunting a brown bear beneficial or dangerous to the expedition? Use logical reasoning to support your opinion.
3. A. What can you infer from the first excerpt about the types of obstacles the expedition encountered?
   B. What obstacle does the phrase "snowy barrier" refer to in the second text?
4. A. How are these two excerpts similar?
   B. How are they different?

PRIMARY SOURCE ANALYSIS

Full Steam Ahead

Read the texts and answer the questions.

Letter to the Editor of the *American Citizen*—published August 20, 1807

I arrived this afternoon at 4 o'clock, in the steam boat, from Albany. As the success of my [steam boat] gives me great hope that such boats may be rendered of much importance to my country...

On Thursday, at 9 o'clock in the morning, I left Albany [by steam boat], and arrived at the Chancellor's at 6 in the evening. I started thence at 7, and arrived at New York on Friday at 4 in the afternoon; time 30 hours, space run through 150 miles, equal to 5 miles an hour—the whole was...performed by the power of the steam engine.

I am, Sir, Your most obedient, Robert Fulton.

Newspaper article about the Erie Canal *(paraphrased)*

October 26, 1825, the largest canal construction in the world is complete—the Erie Canal connects the Hudson River to the Lake Erie. For the first time, a boat in the Atlantic Ocean can enter New York and travel all the way to the Great Lakes without portage. Travel on waterways will replace land travel because of ease and speed. No longer are the Appalachian Mountains a major obstacle to trade of grains from Ohio to New York. Trade by steam boat on the Erie Canal will cut that time in half or more. The Erie Canal opens the Great Lakes and the West to settlers and traders alike!

1. Write a headline to summarize the main idea of each text.
2. A. What is the common theme between the two texts?
   B. How is the mood or tone of the texts similar or different?
3. A. Make at least 5 inferences about author of the first text.
   B. Why did the he include detailed times and distances in his letter?
4. A. Use a dictionary to define portage.
   B. Use the second text to explain how the Erie Canal overcame the obstacle of portage.
5. Explain the significance of inventions to westward expansion.

The Indian Removal Act

Read the text and answer the questions.

As the United States grew, more and more settlers filled the land of the original 13 colonies. However, Native American tribes already occupied the land, and for many years, they fought over rights to land. Most Americans did not approve of Native American culture and thought "civilized" American settlers could better use the land. Settlers' desire for farmland, as well as the discovery of gold in Georgia, prompted the U.S. government to take action.

In May 1830, Congress passed the Indian Removal Act, and President Andrew Jackson signed it into law. The law allowed the U.S. to remove Native Americans in the Southeast and force them to live on land west of the Mississippi River in what is now Oklahoma.

During the fall and winter of 1838-1839, Jackson's military forces gathered Native Americans from their homelands and forced them to march west on what became known as the "Trail of Tears." The Native American people suffered from bitter cold, starvation, and sickness on the journey. The forced <u>relocation</u> of the Cherokee people from Georgia to Oklahoma was especially brutal. Approx. 4,000 Cherokee people died on the journey. By 1847, almost all the Native Americans in the southeastern U.S. had been removed.

1. A. Use the text to define <u>relocation</u>.
   B. Make inferences from the text to explain why the relocation of Native Americans in the 1830s known as the "Trail of Tears"?
2. Complete the graphic organizer by identifying the key causes and effects of the Indian Removal Act.

Causes → **Indian Removal Act** → **Effects**

Manifest Destiny

Read the text and answer the questions.

Although Americans believed the west was wild, untamed, and uncivilized, in the early 1800s many Americans began to move west, drawn by the desire of a new life and riches.

Americans found the idea of spreading west quite natural. Many believed it was America's natural right, given to the nation by God, to expand the United States across North America. This belief that the U.S. should stretch from Atlantic to Pacific Ocean became known as manifest destiny. Americans believed that they were meant to take this land and build a great American civilization.

In part, manifest destiny came from the opinion of Americans that their lifestyle was superior to that of the Native Americans. Americans believed that Native Americans, like the West, were "uncivilized," wild, and had no rules or government. Many of the first settlers to cross the Mississippi River were missionaries who wanted to teach Native Americans to become more like white Americans, including how to farm, how to dress, and how to worship as Christians. More and more Americans followed, traveling west to settle the land, farm, build new towns, start new businesses, and mine for gold. By 1840, approximately 40 percent of all Americans lived west of the Appalachian Mountains.

1. A. Use the text to define manifest destiny.
   B. Explain the ideas that led to Americans' belief in manifest destiny.
2. A. Explain why the East was considered civilized and the West was considered uncivilized.
   B. Identify three antonyms of the word "civilized" that are used to describe the West.
3. A. How did the idea of manifest destiny affect U.S. settlers?
   B. How did the idea of manifest destiny affect Native Americans?
4. "Was manifest destiny a success?" Write an essay to answer the question. Use logical reasoning, examples, evidence (from the text, outside research, what you learned about Westward Expansion), and inferences you make from your own life to support your response. Edit and proof your essay. Present it to your class.

PRIMARY SOURCE ANALYSIS

American Progress

Look at the painting and answer the questions.

Painting by John Gast 1872, titled American Progress - *Courtesy of Library of Congress*

1. A. What do you notice first? Why? Make 3-5 other observations.
   B. What direction are the people traveling? Why?
   C. What methods of transportation are represented in this painting?

2. A. What is the woman doing in the painting?
   B. Make an educated guess about what this woman represents.

3. The artist has contrasted East and West. Match each word below to whether it describes the **East** or the **West** shown in the painting.

A) __________ light	D) __________ wilderness
B) __________ dark	E) __________ danger
C) __________ cities	F) __________ technology

4. Place a ✓ next to all statements that support the artist's contrast of East and West.
   A) ______ American will bring technology to the West!
   B) ______ The Native Americans of the west are noble men.
   C) ______ It is America's destiny to spread from East to West.

Expansion Quotations

Summarize the meaning of each quotation to complete the chart. Use the completed chart to answer the questions.

19th Century quotations:	What each quote means to me:
"[It is] our manifest destiny to over spread and to possess the whole of the continent which Providence has given us for the development of the great experiment of liberty." *—John O'Sullivan, 1845*	
"If a young man is about to commence in the world ... we say to him publicly and privately, go to the West. There, your capacities are sure to be appreciated and your industry and energy rewarded." *— Horace Greely, 1850*	
"It is America's right to stretch from sea to shining sea. Not only do we have a responsibility to our citizens to gain valuable natural resources we also have a responsibility to civilize this beautiful land." *— Admiral Alfred Thayer Mahan*	

1. What is a common theme shared by all three quotations?
2. What reasons do the authors give for moving West?
3. Does each author characterize manifest destiny as more of a right or responsibility? Explain.

The Oregon Trail

Complete the steps in Parts A, B, and C.

PART A: Use at least two online resources and classroom resources to research the Oregon Trail. Take notes and answer the questions below and at least three questions of your own.

1. A. What is a pioneer? What is the Oregon Trail?
   B. Where did the Oregon Trail begin?
   C. Where did the Oregon Trail end?
   D. Who used the Oregon Trail? Why?
   E. When was the Oregon Trail most heavily used?
   F. How did people travel along the Oregon Trail?

2. A. What landmarks did pioneers see on the Oregon Trail?
   B. Why were landmarks important to pioneers on the Oregon Trail?

PART B: Complete the graphic organizer by identifying the many obstacles pioneers encountered on the Oregon Trail.

PART C: Imagine you are a pioneer in 1844 about to depart on the Oregon Trail. Make a list of all the supplies you think you will need along the way. Think about what food, clothing, and protection you will need to survive the 2,000-mile journey. Explain why each item is important.

READING INFORMATIONAL TEXT

Oregon Boundary Dispute

Use the text and the map to answer the questions.

The Oregon Territory in the northwestern United States was claimed by both British and American fur traders. Rather than dividing or fighting over the land, Great Britain and the U.S. agreed to joint occupation, or sharing the land, in the Treaty of 1818.

In 1844, James K. Polk ran for president with a promise to expand the U.S. westward. He won the election. In 1845, Polk oversaw the admittance of Texas as the 28th state. Polk, like many Americans, also wanted to claim the Oregon Territory all the way to its northern boundary at the latitude line 54 degrees 40 minutes. Great Britain disputed the U.S.'s right to claim the territory.

Polk's political slogan, "54-40 or fight!" threatened war against Great Britain. However, the U.S. entered the Mexican-American War in 1846. In order to avoid fighting two wars at the same time, the U.S. agreed to compromise with Great Britain and both countries signed the Oregon Treaty of 1846. This treaty split the Oregon Territory at the 49th parallel, giving Great Britain the northern part, and the U.S. the southern part.

1. A. Use the text to define joint occupation.
   B. What countries had joint occupation of the Oregon Territory?
   C. Was joint occupation effective? Why or why not?

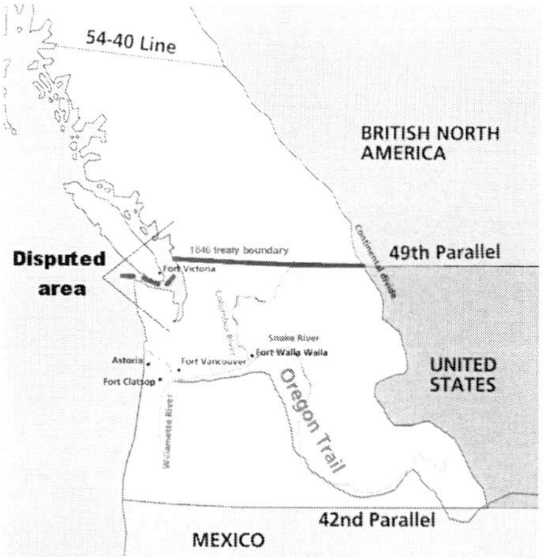

2. A. Explain the meaning of Polk's slogan "54-40 or fight."
   B. What was Great Britain's planned response to Polk?
3. A. Identify the land that was given to the U.S. in the Oregon Treaty and color it blue.
   B. Identify the land that was given to Great Britain in the Oregon Treaty and color it green.
4. What effects did Polk's presidency have on westward expansion? Explain.

SUMMATIVE GRAPHIC ORGANIZER

Mapping Westward Expansion

Use what you know about Westward Expansion and additional resources as needed, to complete the chart. Then use the chart to identify and color each U.S. land acquisition on the map. Then answer the questions.

Land Acquisition	Legislation/ Purchase	Date	Color
Original Territory of the United States			White
Louisiana Territory			Blue
		1819	Yellow
	Annexed by Joint Resolution of Congress		Green
	Oregon Treaty		Purple
		1848	Red
	Bought from Mexico		Orange

1. A. Label the Pacific Ocean and Atlantic Ocean.
   B. What line serves as a boundary between the United States and Canada? When was this line established?
   C. What river acted as the western boundary for the U.S. in the late 1700s? What caused this to change?
   D. What significant benefit did the Oregon Territory give the U.S.?

2. Compare and contrast a physical map of the U.S. today with the westward expansion map to answer these questions:
   A. During westward expansion, which U.S. geographical features helped form the boundaries of territories?
   B. Make at least two generalizations by comparing the borders of land acquisitions with the borders of individual states today.
   C. Explain how the events of westward expansion helped to shape the boundaries of the United States today.

3. Read the 1845 quotation by John O'Sullivan:

"[It is] our manifest destiny to over spread and to possess the whole of the continent which Providence has given us for the development of the great experiment of liberty."

Was John O'Sullivan's statement of manifest destiny realized or not? Cite evidence from the map and/or chart to support your answer.

Slavery Expands Westward

Read the text and answer the questions.

As Americans moved West, so did the slave trade. The expansion of slavery to western territories sparked a heated debate between Northern free states and Southern slave states. Abolitionist groups feared that slavery would spread west. Pro-slavery groups saw an opportunity to start big businesses on large slave plantations in the West.

When a Western territory applied to become a state, the territory chose between becoming a free state or a slave state. The balance of power between free and slave states was delicate. Two famous compromises, the Missouri Compromise and the Compromise of 1850, managed to keep peace between the states by admitting some states as slave states and some as free states.

1. What effects did westward expansion have on slavery? What is the relationship between the expansion of slavery and the Civil War?

2. Analyze each statement and identify whether it **most likely** expresses the point of view of a Southern slave owner or a Northern abolitionist.

   _____________ A man has the right to take his "property" with him to a new territory.
   _____________ Slavery is a disease. We must stop it before it infects the entire nation!
   _____________ The servant will of course want to follow the master into the West.

3. Use an online resource to research the Missouri Compromise and the Compromise of 1850, and complete each graphic organizer.

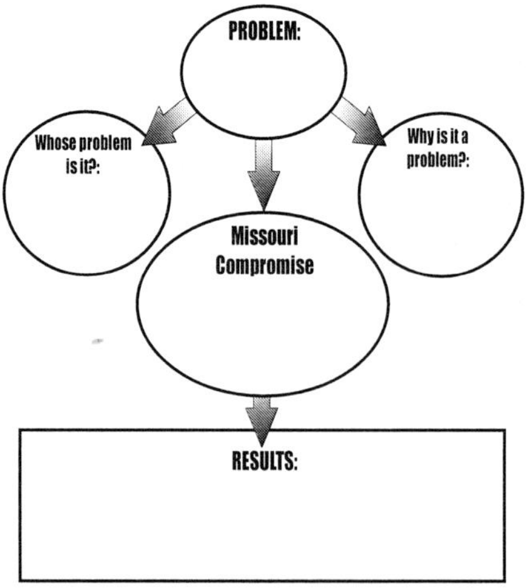

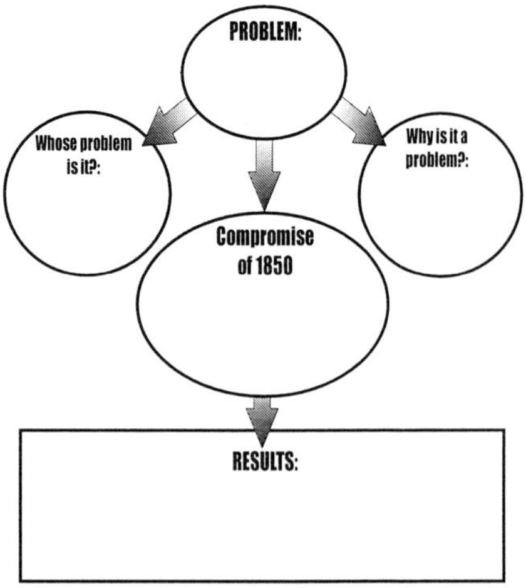

Texas: The 28th State

Read the text and answer the questions.

In the 1820s, Mexico won its independence from Spain. The new Mexican government, led by Santa Anna, wanted to settle the large areas of land in what is now Texas. To settle the land more quickly, Mexico offered large grants of land to Americans. Many Americans were eager for cheap land and settled in Mexico alongside the native Tejanos (Mexican settlers).

Americans and Tejanos lived in peace for a time, but problems soon arose. Mexico outlawed slavery in 1929, but many American settlers brought slaves to Mexico to work on ranches. By the 1830s, Americans and their slaves outnumbered the Tejanos in Texas. Americans refused to follow the Mexican government's ban on slavery.

In 1836, Stephen E. Austin and other Texan leaders claimed Texas and declared independence from Mexico. To stop them, Santa Anna marched the Mexican army to Texas. Santa Anna attacked a small group of Texan rebels at a small fort called the Alamo. After 13 days of battle, Santa Anna's army captured the Alamo, killing the 150+ Americans within the fort.

Six weeks later, a military group of Texans killed more than 600 Mexican soldiers and captured Santa Anna, shouting, "Remember the Alamo!" Santa Anna was forced to sign the Treaty of Valesco, which gave Texas its independence. Texan leaders hoped to join the United States, but Texas did not become a U.S. state until 1845. In the nine years between Texas' independence and being admitted as a U.S. state, Texas was its own country!

1. A. Why did Mexico give Texas land to Americans?
   B. How did this decision affect the future of Texas?
2. List 3 causes of tension between Americans and Mexicans.
3. What can you infer about the Texas military group's reaction to events at the Alamo? Cite evidence from the text to support your answer.
4. Use the text to number the following events in chronological order:
   _____Texas gains its independence from Mexico
   _____Mexico wins independence from Spain
   _____Texas declares independence

MAP ACTIVITY

Acquisition of Mexican Land

Read the text, look at the map, and answer the questions.

The Treaty of Guadalupe-Hidalgo officially ended the Mexican-American War (1846-1848). As a result, the United States gained the Mexican Cession and the land disputed between Texas and Mexico.

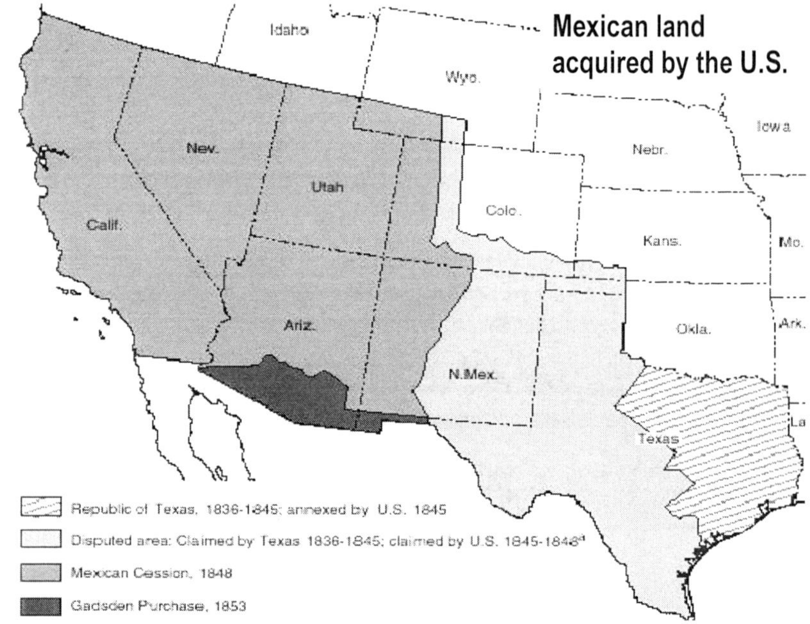

1. A. What is the primary purpose of this map?
   B. What do the shaded areas represent?
   C. What other information does this map provide?
2. Between which years did the U.S. officially acquire land from Mexico?
3. Color the map with a crayon or marker to show the land the U.S. acquired through the Treaty of Guadalupe-Hidalgo.
4. **True** or **False**: The Treaty of Guadalupe-Hidalgo set the southern boundaries for the state of Texas today.
5. How did the Treaty of Guadalupe-Hidalgo affect westward expansion?

READING INFORMATIONAL TEXT

California Gold Rush

Read the texts and answer the questions.

The discovery of gold in California's Sacramento Valley in 1848 started the California Gold Rush. The frenzy for gold encouraged thousands of Americans to settle in the Western territories, and forever changed the population of California. As news of the discovery spread, over 300,000 people migrated or immigrated to California. Americans from the East traveled over land and by sea and were called the 49ers. Quickly constructed mining towns, or "boomtowns," were built seemingly overnight. From outside the U.S., people from Mexico, Peru, Chile, China, Ireland, and even Germany came seeking fortunes to take back home. But, few immigrants returned home. Most immigrants settled in the Western territories. By 1858, more than $2 billion worth of precious metal had been mined from California.

Excerpt from the diary of a gold miner in 1849:

"Everything was lively in Stockton. Buildings of all kinds were being rushed... There were many cloth houses, tents of all kinds, and shacks of every description. The price for houses was [very expensive]... People were flocking to the mines, some walking with their blankets strapped on their backs... some on mule back; but all were trying to reach the gold district. Many came back and reported the whole thing a hoax and a failure."

1. A. Use a dictionary to define migrate and immigrate.
   B. Which people migrated to California? Which people immigrated?
2. What effect did the Gold Rush have on the population of California?
3. List several characteristics of "boomtowns" and explain why "boomtowns" had those characteristics.
4. A. What is being described in the second text?
   B. Cite evidence from the second text that supports the description "frenzy for gold" in the first text.
   C. What can you infer about the Gold Rush from the sentence, "Many came back and reported the whole thing a hoax and a failure"?

COMPARISON OF PRIMARY SOURCES

Chinese in the West

From 1848-1852, Chinese immigrants came in large numbers to the American West. They helped build the Transcontinental Railroad and mined for gold in California.

Read the text, look at the political cartoon, and answer the questions.

"These people form a peaceable and hardworking class of our population, but are of very little service or benefit...to the state.... Rice, their great staple, they generally bring over with them in vast quantities, and when a Chinaman amasses a small amount of cash, he immediately returns home to the 'flowery land'."
—*Three Years Residence in California*, by William Perkins

"Pacific Chivalry: Encouragement to Chinese Immigrants" by Thomas Nast *Courtesy of Library of Congress*

1. A. Describe Perkins' opinion of Chinese immigrants.
   B. What reasons does he provide to support his opinion?
   C. What is meant by "flowery land" in the text?
   D. What can you infer from the text about Chinese immigrants' reasons for coming to California?

A. Who do the two people in the cartoon represent?
   B. Use a dictionary to define <u>chivalry</u> and <u>encouragement</u>.
   C. Explain the author's purpose for the title of the cartoon.
   D. What can you infer from the cartoon about Californians' treatment of Chinese immigrants?
   E. What can you infer from the cartoon about Nast's point of view?

2. A. Draw a political cartoon to illustrate a contemporary issue today.
   B. Provide a descriptive analysis of your cartoon and what it means.

Pacific Railroad Act of 1862

Use the text and complete the graphic organizer.

By 1850, more than 9,000 miles of railroad tracks connected the states east of the Mississippi River. Railroads enabled interstate trade, and created a better network of travel, communication, and business in the East. Travel to the West, however, was still limited. Pioneers braved the risky and difficult six-month journey in covered wagons along the Oregon and California trails. Other fortune-seekers took the six-month journey by boat around South America.

President Lincoln encouraged westward expansion. He saw the railroads as an opportunity to greatly improve trade with the West and strengthen the Union. In 1862, Congress passed the Pacific Railroad Act, and President Lincoln signed it into law. This act gave large land grants to railroad companies to build a transcontinental railroad from East to West.

The Union Pacific Railroad Company began construction in Council Bluffs, Iowa, on the eastern side of the Missouri River, and built west. The Central Pacific Railroad Company began construction in Sacramento, California, and built east. Their goal was to join in the middle. On May 10, 1869, the two railroads joined at Promontory, Utah. Now, the United States was connected by railroad from the Atlantic Ocean to the Pacific Ocean!

1. A. The prefix "inter" means "between." Use the prefix and the text to define interstate trade.
   B. How did the East benefit from interstate railroads in the 1850s?
2. A. The prefix "trans" means "across." Use the prefix and the text to define transcontinental.
   B. What was the purpose of the transcontinental railroad?
   C. Why was the Pacific Railroad Act necessary?
3. Describe the relationship between the transcontinental railroad and manifest destiny.
4. Predict how the transcontinental railroad affected each of the following:
   A. wagon trains B. interstate trade C. western settlement

The Homestead Act

Read the texts and answer the questions.

The Homestead Act of 1862 was passed by Congress to encourage land development in the West. Qualified homesteaders were required to claim, live on, and develop 160 acres of land for a minimum of five years. Close to 500,000 homesteaders would receive over 80 million acres by the start of 1900. Nearly 10% of the United States was settled with land grants from in the Homestead Act.

The following text is a first-person narrative of Jenny, a Nebraska homesteader.

Jessup was almost grown by the time we moved to Nebraska. Mary was born shortly after. We took our chances on the homestead because Danny wasn't making enough money in the mill. He said there was a chance for him in the West—nobody to say he couldn't.

I didn't say he couldn't, but nature gives and nature takes. The first winter, half our mules died from cold. Spring brought rain, wildflowers, and softened the hard soil. The ground was ready for planting crops, but our first harvest produced very little. We lived by hunting wild animals. The second year's harvest was plentiful, and we all worked hard for every bit of food we had.

We built our house at the base of a slight rise near a creek. The rise protects the house from howling winds at night, and the creek is good for washing and drinking. Without trees or stone anywhere in sight, Danny and Jessup cut sod bricks made of grass and earth. One by one, we stacked the walls high against the slope, and cut into the hillside. Danny dug a ditch from the stream to the crops, and the mules stay close to the creek in hot summers.

1. Make at least three inferences about the author of the second text. Cite evidence from the text to support each inference.
2. Explain the relationship between the Homestead Act and the author of the second text.
3. A. List at least 5 obstacles homesteaders faced on the prairie.
   B. Describe how homesteaders overcame those obstacles.
4. List the requirements of the Homestead Act and explain their purpose. Cite evidence from both texts to support your answer.

POINT OF VIEW

Chinese Exclusion Act

Read the text and quotations and answer the questions.

Chinese immigrants were influential in westward expansion: they helped build the Transcontinental Railroad, and they labored as miners, farmers, machine-operators, cooks, repairmen, and other useful trades. Economic downturn and the completion of the transcontinental railroad left many Americans without jobs. Competition with the Chinese immigrants for jobs, as well as cultural differences, led to the Chinese Exclusion Act, which banned Chinese people from immigrating to the U.S. from 1882 to 1943.

> (Chinese) people in this country have been peaceable, law-abiding and industrious... They have not displaced white laborers from their positions, but have simply multiplied the industrial enterprise of this country.
>
> –Memorial (a written document) from leaders of the "Six Companies" (6 Chinese organizations) to President Grant, 1876

> We have this day to choose... whether our legislation shall be in the interest of the American free labor or the servile labor from China... You cannot work a man who must have beef and bread... alongside a man who can live on rice. It cannot be done!
>
> –James G. Blaine, Senator from Maine, Speech to Congress, 1882

1. A. Summarize the point of view described in the first quotation.
   B. Summarize the point of view described in the second quotation.
2. Identify who or what is being described in the second quotation:
   A. "legislation"
   B. "the interest of American free labor"
   C. "a man who must have beef and bread"
   D. "a man who can live on rice"
3. A. Why did Americans think the Chinese Exclusion Act was necessary? Cite evidence from the quotations to support your answer.
   B. What other underlying factors led to the Act?
4. A. What were the immediate results of the Chinese Exclusion Act?
   B. What can you infer were the long term results of the Chinese Exclusion Act?

Westward Expansion

Complete the graphic organizer for each person, describing their role or influence in westward expansion.

People	Who am I?	What did I do?
Thomas Jefferson		
Meriwether Lewis and William Clark		
Andrew Jackson		
James K. Polk		
Abraham Lincoln		
Thomas Nast		
Robert Fulton		
Santa Anna		

Words of Expansion

Use a dictionary and other resources to complete the graphic organizer for each word or phrase.

acquisition
annexation
canal
cession
claim
empresario
expedition
frontier
homestead
immigrant
Indian reservation
manifest destiny
migration
mission
pioneer
steamboat
territory
treaty
wagon train

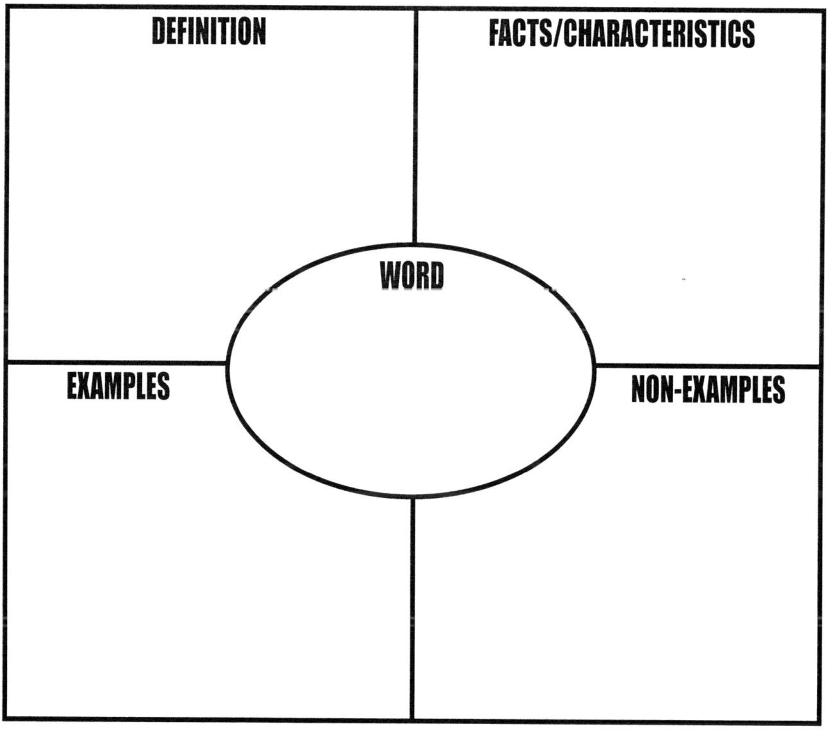

Correlations to Common Core State Standards

For your convenience, correlations are listed page-by-page, and for the entire book!

This book is correlated to the Common Core State Standards for English Language Arts grades 3-8, and to Common Core State Standards for Literacy in History, Science, & Technological Subjects grades 6-8.

Correlations are highlighted in gray.

	READING	WRITING	LANGUAGE	SPEAKING & LISTENING
	Includes: RI: Reading Informational Text; RH: Reading History/Social Studies	*Includes:* W: Writing; WHST: Writing History/Social Studies, Science, & Technical Subjects	*Includes:* L: Language; LF: Language Foundational Skills	*Includes:* SL: Speaking & Listening
PAGE #				
2-3	RI RH . 1 2 3 4 5 6 7 8 9 10	W WHST . 1 2 3 4 5 6 7 8 9 10	L LF . 1 2 3 4 5 6	SL . 1 2 3 4 5 6
4	RI RH . 1 2 3 4 5 6 7 8 9 10	W WHST . 1 2 3 4 5 6 7 8 9 10	L LF . 1 2 3 4 5 6	SL . 1 2 3 4 5 6
5	RI RH . 1 2 3 4 5 6 7 8 9 10	W WHST . 1 2 3 4 5 6 7 8 9 10	L LF . 1 2 3 4 5 6	SL . 1 2 3 4 5 6
6	RI RH . 1 2 3 4 5 6 7 8 9 10	W WHST . 1 2 3 4 5 6 7 8 9 10	L LF . 1 2 3 4 5 6	SL . 1 2 3 4 5 6
7	RI RH . 1 2 3 4 5 6 7 8 9 10	W WHST . 1 2 3 4 5 6 7 8 9 10	L LF . 1 2 3 4 5 6	SL . 1 2 3 4 5 6
8	RI RH . 1 2 3 4 5 6 7 8 9 10	W WHST . 1 2 3 4 5 6 7 8 9 10	L LF . 1 2 3 4 5 6	SL . 1 2 3 4 5 6
9	RI RH . 1 2 3 4 5 6 7 8 9 10	W WHST . 1 2 3 4 5 6 7 8 9 10	L LF . 1 2 3 4 5 6	SL . 1 2 3 4 5 6
10	RI RH . 1 2 3 4 5 6 7 8 9 10	W WHST . 1 2 3 4 5 6 7 8 9 10	L LF . 1 2 3 4 5 6	SL . 1 2 3 4 5 6
11	RI RH . 1 2 3 4 5 6 7 8 9 10	W WHST . 1 2 3 4 5 6 7 8 9 10	L LF . 1 2 3 4 5 6	SL . 1 2 3 4 5 6
12-13	RI RH . 1 2 3 4 5 6 7 8 9 10	W WHST . 1 2 3 4 5 6 7 8 9 10	L LF . 1 2 3 4 5 6	SL . 1 2 3 4 5 6
14	RI RH . 1 2 3 4 5 6 7 8 9 10	W WHST . 1 2 3 4 5 6 7 8 9 10	L LF . 1 2 3 4 5 6	SL . 1 2 3 4 5 6
15	RI RH . 1 2 3 4 5 6 7 8 9 10	W WHST . 1 2 3 4 5 6 7 8 9 10	L LF . 1 2 3 4 5 6	SL . 1 2 3 4 5 6
16	RI RH . 1 2 3 4 5 6 7 8 9 10	W WHST . 1 2 3 4 5 6 7 8 9 10	L LF . 1 2 3 4 5 6	SL . 1 2 3 4 5 6
17	RI RH . 1 2 3 4 5 6 7 8 9 10	W WHST . 1 2 3 4 5 6 7 8 9 10	L LF . 1 2 3 4 5 6	SL . 1 2 3 4 5 6
18	RI RH . 1 2 3 4 5 6 7 8 9 10	W WHST . 1 2 3 4 5 6 7 8 9 10	L LF . 1 2 3 4 5 6	SL . 1 2 3 4 5 6
19	RI RH . 1 2 3 4 5 6 7 8 9 10	W WHST . 1 2 3 4 5 6 7 8 9 10	L LF . 1 2 3 4 5 6	SL . 1 2 3 4 5 6
20	RI RH . 1 2 3 4 5 6 7 8 9 10	W WHST . 1 2 3 4 5 6 7 8 9 10	L LF . 1 2 3 4 5 6	SL . 1 2 3 4 5 6
21	RI RH . 1 2 3 4 5 6 7 8 9 10	W WHST . 1 2 3 4 5 6 7 8 9 10	L LF . 1 2 3 4 5 6	SL . 1 2 3 4 5 6
22	RI RH . 1 2 3 4 5 6 7 8 9 10	W WHST . 1 2 3 4 5 6 7 8 9 10	L LF . 1 2 3 4 5 6	SL . 1 2 3 4 5 6
23	RI RH . 1 2 3 4 5 6 7 8 9 10	W WHST . 1 2 3 4 5 6 7 8 9 10	L LF . 1 2 3 4 5 6	SL . 1 2 3 4 5 6
COMPLETE BOOK	RI RH . 1 2 3 4 5 6 7 8 9 10	W WHST . 1 2 3 4 5 6 7 8 9 10	L LF . 1 2 3 4 5 6	SL . 1 2 3 4 5 6

For the complete Common Core standard identifier, combine your grade + "." + letter code above + "." + number code above.

In addition to the correlations indicated here, the activities may be adapted or expanded to align to additional standards and to meet the diverse needs of your unique students!